Thank you for
your dedication to
the Youth and Children
of our community.
First Baptist

D0007893

devotionals for teachers

devotionals for teachers

Nelle A. Vander Ark

BAKER BOOK HOUSE
Grand Rapids, Michigan

Printed in the United States of America

Passages from (NEB) *The New English Bible,* © the Delegates
of the Oxford University Press and the Syndics of the Cambridge University Press, 1961, 1970, are reprinted by permission of Cambridge University Press. Quotations from
(NIV) the *New International Version,* © 1973 by New York
Bible Society International are used with permission. Permission was given to use material from (Berkeley) *Modern
Language New Testament—The New Berkeley Version in Modern English* © 1945, 59, 69 by Zondervan Publishing House.
The National Council of the Churches of Christ gave permission to use passages from (RSV) the *Revised Standard
Version Bible.*

*Dedicated to
the memory of
MY MOTHER,
my first teacher*

May my teaching drop as the rain,
My speech distil as the dew,
As the gentle rain upon the tender grass,
And as the showers upon the herb.
For I will proclaim the name of the Lord.
Ascribe greatness to our God!
Deuteronomy 32:2-3, RSV

CONTENTS

Introduction

I wrote these meditations for all kinds of teachers and also for other people who relish a variety of food for thought plus some firming-up exercises for the soul. As I wrote each piece, I tried to think of ways to carry such thoughts into the classroom and into life as a whole—to suggest how contemplation on the ways of God could become part of one's being and thus part of his teaching and living. It is fairly easy to have a "time of devotions;" it is hard to live our devotions throughout each day, to steadily "exercise ourselves unto godliness" and to "pray without ceasing." This book is intended to aid such exercise.

I suggest that you:

1. Page through the book and get a feel for its general content and approach.

2. Read a few selections that most appeal to you. Savor them a bit.

3. Choose one that particularly strikes you. Read the Scripture passages recommended for a fuller development of the thought.

4. Reflect. Think. Pray. Enjoy!

5. Dream of ways to implement within the next twenty-four hours something of the thoughts that come to you. There is nothing magic about the number 24 except that it represents one full day and night. And I've found that usually my ideas produce more fruit when planted promptly. You may find that some of the meditations will carry over into more than a day or even a week.

6. Keep a simple record for yourself, such as: Thought, Idea for Action, Result, Next Step.

One of my favorite gifts is a little black notebook a new friend gave me some months ago. On the cover she penned: Things Worth Remembering. Inside she wrote: "This is so you won't have to scribble on every blank square of church bulletin or whatever. Just tuck it in your purse and whip it out when the notion seizes you." I recommend the scribbling habit to you, and sincerely hope that this book may give you some irresistible "seizures."

1

An Invitation to Joy

Scripture: Psalm 34

"Come, my children, listen to me:
I will teach you the fear of the Lord" (Ps. 34:11, NEB).

Today is new. You and I greet the Lord in the freshness of the morning, and we want to meet our students with vigor and cheer. We can. We have an invitation to hand out to them—like inviting them to a party. We can say, "Listen, I've got something exciting to tell you this morning. So, gather round, listen, and I'll tell you about it."

In that spirit of invitation, excitement, and expectancy, the Lord teaches us and gives us direction for teaching others. The words are simple: "Come, my children, listen to me."

The writer of this psalm, as well as the writer of the Book of Proverbs, knew the secret—the indispensable first step—in real teaching: LISTEN! Read the psalm once again and just sit back and listen. Note the appeal to all your senses—hear, look, taste, see, delight, enjoy! Then, be on the alert for fresh ways and the many, little ways in which you hear God today, taste His goodness, and enjoy Him.

And then, rather than seeking to exercise all the cautions we often set up in the minds of children by undue emphasis on such songs as: "O, be careful, little hands, what you do . . .", catch the spirit of Psalm 34: BLESS! PRAISE! EXALT THE LORD!

> USE my heart, USE my mind, USE my hand
> To scatter love and sunshine through the land,
> The love of Christ display,
> Helping someone day by day.
> Use my heart, use my mind, use my hand.
> Thomas Dorsey

2

Child of God

Scripture: I John 2:28—3:3

> *"Here and now . . . we are God's children"* (I John 3:2, NEB).

"Identity crisis!" We hear the cry all around us. Take the above text, put it on your tongue, and let it act as a lozenge and as a tonic for you and for those whom you teach. Meditate on it for a few minutes.

Christians know who they are. They also know that the present—the "here and now"—is very important. We must know about the past, but we cannot dwell there. We must prepare for the future, but we cannot really live beyond today.

Rejoice in the certainty that "here and now we are God's children." We have identity and purpose. We are *alive now*! May God show us how to be alive for Him—to enter into life today with joy and vigor.

This chorus, old and familiar, has often helped me keep my perspective:

> I'm a child of the King,
> A child of the King;
> With Jesus my Savior
> I'm a child of the King.

Suggestion: Make a Bible bookmark for yourself (and for your students if conditions allow). Take a ribbon (1 inch wide, 6 inches long) and with a felt-tip pen write: I BELONG TO GOD. That thought will give you (and your students) substance for the greatest comfort in life and the most reliable guide for all decision-making.

3

Kings and Queens

Scripture: Galatians 3:26—4:7

> *"You are therefore no longer a slave but a son, and if a son, then also by God's own act an heir" (Gal. 4:7, NEB).*

> O happy land, whose sons in youth,
> In sturdy strength and noble truth,
> Like plants in vigor spring;
> Whose daughters fair, a queenly race,
> Are like the cornerstones that grace
> The palace of a king.

> First stanza of metrical version of Psalm 144, *The Psalter,* 1912

Many of us know that song and have sung it often. Sing it again this morning. Then think of your position in this world. Sons and daughters of the living God are co-heirs with Jesus. Wow! What a thought! Because of Christ's work we have received our inheritance. We have work to do—an estate to manage.

How can we prove ourselves to be responsible, effective caretakers of the land assigned to us? Well, we have a class to teach. We'll need to plan carefully how we're going to carry out God's business today. Try listing what needs doing, in order, and then decide what materials you need to do each task. Steadily work toward more and more specifics.

But always remember your stance—kings and queens. C. S. Lewis said it so well in *The Lion, the Witch, and the Wardrobe:* "And now I anoint you kings and queens of Narnia. Remember, once a king or a queen . . . always a king or a queen. Bear it well!"

Suggestion: Watch your posture today. Stand tall. You have steel in your spine.

4

Know Their Names

Scripture: Psalm 147:1-7; John 10:1-15

> *"He . . . numbers the stars one by one and names them*
> *one and all" (Ps. 147:4, NEB).*
> *"I have called you by name . . . "(Isa. 43:1b, NEB).*
> *". . . He calls his own sheep by name . . ." (John 10:3, NEB).*
> *"I know my own sheep and my sheep know me"*
> *(John 10:14b, NEB).*

This past semester I was privileged to have in one of my classes a very perceptive woman who had discontinued a fine career in nursing and had chosen to take some more college work "to fill in some of the blanks" in her life. Her contributions to the class showed that she had "lived" much more than the usual college student, and her out-of-class comments encouraged me from time to time. She often noted practices that I had been working at for years but had not thought of these qualities as being especially noteworthy. But, I'm grateful for Dorothy's remarks. They brightened my days and also gave me ideas for strengthening you in the classroom and in all relationships.

One quality Dorothy pointed out was that I knew every student's name (though I had over 100 each semester) and always addressed them by name. All I could say to her compliment was, "Thank you and thank God for leading me to see the importance of names and helping me persevere in learning to know each student by name."

I know many of you discipline yourselves in this practice; others may need a bit of prodding to see its importance. Knowing names is God-like. God knows the names of every star (Ps. 147:4), and He also knows the name of every one of His children and calls them by name (John 10:3, 14). Almost unbelievable, isn't it? But it's true. I invite you to note times recorded in Scripture when God addressed men directly—by a voice, by men, and angels, and in Christ. Note the "nouns of direct

16

address"—the names spoken.

So, if we desire to be "more like the Master," we must learn peoples' names and call people by name. There is nothing that a teacher can do that reveals more personal interest in another than to greet him and to speak to him by name.

Learning names is a discipline, but *discipline* and *disciple* come from the same root, you see. And that root is more than a linguistic phenomenon. That root is God's way to make His "school" grow.

As a disciple of God and as a teacher in discipleship, practice the discipline of knowing your students by name. You will find a surprising delight in it because God delights in those who seek to be like Him.

How can you know His delight, His approval? Practice His ways and soon you will know beyond a doubt (perhaps by student feedback) that God is saying to you, "That's good. I appreciate the way you know your students. Keep going!"

> My Lord, I do not ask to stand
> As king or prince of high degree.
> I only pray that hand in hand
> A child and I may come to Thee.
>
> As step by step we tread the way,
> Trusting, and confident, and free—
> A child and I shall day by day,
> Find sweet companionship with Thee.
> Norman E. Richardson
> Florence I. Judson-Bradley

5

Healing in the Air

Scripture: I John 3:18-24; 4:7-21; Ephesians 4:11-16

*"This is my commandment to you:
love one another" (John 15:17, NEB).*

I have a growing concern about Christian teaching, and I know many of you share my concern. It is simply: we preach love but we teach competition. Some of our grading systems, for example, tend to foster the spirit of "everybody for himself" rather than to create and sustain a spirit of mutual helpfulness and responsibility.

How can we teach others that we are indeed our brothers' keepers? How can we teach love and so begin to implement the most basic command of Christ and the foundation of all Christian living—"love one another"?

One way is to identify a gift or a strength in each student and build on it. In educational language, this step is sometimes referred to as: determining or assessing your potential for teaching. Basic to this search for potential is an intimate acquaintance between teacher and student. There is a further step, however, that is often overlooked: students have to learn to know and appreciate each one of their classmates and assume responsibility for one another.

We have so much student information on record in the office; we elicit so little live data from our students and record it on our hearts and the hearts of fellow students. We spend hours, sometimes days, marking papers and faithfully "keeping book." I wonder what would happen if we cut that time in half and spent the other half in getting to know one another, to identify strengths, and to invent ways to help one another—to become more and more "all one body—building itself up in love."

What would happen if we'd really quit thinking as the Greeks thought and doing as the Romans did and instead took Paul's words in Ephesians 4 (and also Romans 12) as the basis for our teaching and for all of life? "And these were his gifts; some to be . . . teachers, to equip God's people for work in his service, to the building up of the body of Christ" (Eph. 4:11, 12, NEB). And then, what would happen if we built on that basis every day and looked upon every student and colleague as an indispensable working part of Christ's body—no person too small and no one independent of the other, but all working together and each one helping others to realize their God-given potential. Might we then not see a whole body grow, not just individual people? When we see this kind of growth, we will know that we are teaching what the Lord commands: "Love one another."

Recommended reading: For understanding more of the substance of self-less love, read Thomas Merton's book *No Man Is an Island* (Image Books Edition), published by Doubleday & Co., Inc. A few quotes may whet your appetite:

> Love seeks only one thing: the good of the one loved. p. 19

> Charity makes me seek far more than the satisfaction of my own desires, even though they be aimed at another's good. It must also make me an instrument of God's Providence in their lives. . . . My will must be the instrument of God's will in helping them create their own destiny. p. 20

> Charity is not hungry. It is . . . a feast in which we are nourished by serving others rather than by feeding ourselves. p.26

6

Walk Together, Children

Scripture: Gal. 5:13-26

> *"If we live by the Spirit,*
> *let us also walk*
> *by the Spirit" (Gal. 5:25, RSV).*

Recently I heard one of my students, a delightful "songbird," sing a modern gospel song that made my spirit soar with hers:

> Walk together, children;
> Walk together.
> Walk together and your troubles seem lighter.
> Just walk together, talk together,
> Pray together, and your way seems brighter.
> Just walk, walk together, children,
>   each step of the way.
>
> James Voyer

How can we teachers walk together today? It may be a physical hike, walking to school with someone or tramping through the woods after hours. Or, the walk may be a symbol of other "togetherness" exercises which we may not recognize as ways of walking "by the Spirit" and yet these walks are so vital to the buoyancy of the human spirit and to enjoyment of our work.

Do we "walk together" and do we "talk together" in the teachers' lounge or in faculty meetings? Do we "walk together" with our students? Do we pray together as we "walk together"? Are we missing out on certain blessedness in our work and in our "walk with the Lord" because we miss opportunities to "walk together" as co-laborers with God?

"Walk together, children, each step of the way," and you will have a good day.

7

Refreshments Will Be Served

Scripture: Philemon

> ". . . *The hearts of the saints*
> *have been refreshed through you"* (*Philem. 7b, RSV*).

Refreshing people were important to Paul. He recorded the specific ministry of two of them—Philemon and Onesiphorus. Philemon refreshed many believers by serving the church in his house. Onesiphorus came all the way from Ephesus to find Paul in Rome and refresh him when Paul was a chained prisoner there (II Tim. 1:16).

Refresh yourself this morning by thinking of ways to refresh others. Go over your class roll name by name, reflect on a few names each day, and then consider how you might refresh each student and your class as a whole. Then, broaden your base and think of one way to refresh a colleague. Perhaps he would welcome an invitation to go out for lunch with you.

Walk to school briskly, and enter your classroom as if you had a sign on your door: Refreshments will be served here today.

And at the end of the day, may you hear the Lord say to you (perhaps through some person): "The hearts of the saints have been refreshed through you."

> O Lord, refresh us by Thy grace;
> Revive and quicken all our powers,
> As failing streams are made to flow
> Replenished by abundant showers.

8

Get Rid of Negative Attitudes

Scripture: Hebrews 12

> *"See to it . . . that no one cultivates a root of bitterness"* (Heb. 12:15, Berkeley).
> *". . . let us get rid of every impediment"* (Heb. 12:17, Berkeley).

Several weeks ago I had an encounter with a student. He questioned my position, and in the process "hit me over the head" with Biblical references. Outwardly, I was unruffled and told him calmly and rationally how I thought we could resolve the problem. Inwardly, I was seething and "in the stubbornness of my heart," I cultivated "a root of bitterness," and resented that young man for days. That attitude interfered with my work. It blinded me to all the goodness the Lord had provided for me in other relationships each day. It robbed me of joy. I detected a withering spirit within me.

Then, the Lord brought me to my senses as He does time and time again. I read Hebrews 12. I began to look to the life of Christ. How did He cope with such matters? He prayed for those who longed to kill him: "Father, forgive them for they know not what they do." And I asked God to give me grace to pray that prayer sincerely. He gave me such grace. In fact, He helped me see that I didn't even have to work so hard at putting bitterness and wrath away. I just had to *let* it be put away (Eph. 4:31) by the renewing power of the Spirit.

It was a tremendous relief and a blessed growth experience. I received new zest for my work and saw clearly the next step for my life: "And be kind to one another, tenderhearted, forgiving one another, as God in Christ forgave you" (Eph. 4:32, RSV). And I knew with joy and confidence that God would give me what I needed to take that step, too.

Recommended exercise: Call to mind someone who has hurt you deeply. Take his hand, look him in the eye, and say, "The grace of the Lord Jesus Christ . . . be with you" (II Cor. 13:14).

9

Be Fired with a New Idea

Scripture: Ephesians 5:15-20

". . . Be filled with the Spirit and addressing one another in psalms and hymns, and spiritual songs, singing and making melody to the Lord with all your heart" (Eph. 5:18b-19, RSV).

Teaching is a gift—a gift of the Spirit (Rom. 12:6-7). And the Spirit Himself nourishes that gift. "Thy Spirit, O Lord, makes life to abound" (metrical version of Ps. 104:30). Now it remains for us to seek out new and fruitful ways to exercise it.

True, the work of the Spirit is mysterious but recognizable. To know more of His power and His amazingly stimulating ways of working in our lives and in our students, we ought to pray expectantly when we pray for the Spirit to work in us. Try praying "with your eyes open" and with your hands ready to move when He puts an idea into your head. When we pray that way and look for ways to implement our prayers, we will discover how it is possible to "never flag in zeal, be aglow with the Spirit . . ." (Rom. 12:11a, RSV).

Let me illustrate. In teaching poetry appreciation last month, I came upon an article about the poetry in the Psalms and suggestions for having a psalm-writing bee. Since I have been brought up in the psalms and recognize their cross-cultural sweep and impact, I began work on psalm reading and writing in my poetry class. It proved to be a series of delightful experiences—of learning the form of Hebraic poetry, of writing our own psalms, sharing them in class, and even overflowing into a psalm festival as a chapel service—choral readings, readings of students' products, and a grand finale of Dutch psalm singing in the majestic chorale style. What fun! (And it was especially thrilling to see how students of another background rejoiced in sharing my heritage and in helping to preserve it.)

This psalm was written by one of my students. May it be a blessing to you and perhaps fire you with a new idea:

Psalm for Dependence

The Lord pours out His blessings upon me;
His manifold goodness He ceaselessly sends.
It comes in such bounty,
In such bounty that I can hardly take it in
—Just as rain cannot completely saturate the red clay
But still persists
                in
                        coming down upon it.

What can I say to You LORD, the Faithful;
Which words to praise Your name most holy?
Who, God, exalts You,
Exalts You with adequate praise?

O bless the LORD in joyous moments,
On Him rely from day to day.
Depend on Him when life flows rightly:
            when the tongue is satisfied,
                and the belly is full;
            when supplication is heard;
            when friends grow fonder and a
                beloved's countenance glows;
            when work is not toilsome—when it
                becomes as play;
            when this young steward is rewarded
                for her allotted time wisely used.

O let me ne'er forget to thank You,
Dearest companion,
LORD of my life.
May I always rest
In the perfection of your coherent design,
In the mysterious outworkings of Your decrees.

Peggy Edwards

24

10

Farm According to the Land You Have

Scripture: Psalm 37

> *"Trust in the Lord and do good; settle in the land and find safe pasture"* *(Ps. 37:3, NEB).*

I thank God for my rural background and my experiences in farming. So many references in the field of literature and many figures in the Bible seem richer to me because I know a bit about farming. But whether or not you have farmed, the maxim that heads this page applies to your daily living by faith and demonstrating that faith in your teaching.

"Farm according to the land you have." Where is your land located? What kind of soil and resources do you have to work with? How much land do you have? How can you with your particular talents and limitations best manage your assigned acreage so that you and your students become ever more fruitful?

These and many more are basic questions for living by faith —the only living that God recognizes as "really living." The psalmist gives us much basic direction in answering these questions. According to Psalm 37:3, the first step is: "Trust in the Lord." I don't profess to know all that that means. Certainly it means, in part, that I must recognize that God gave me a work to do and a place to do it. And, believing that my work is God-given, I can go ahead with Him confidently, happily, and take the next step: "do good." Say those two words to yourself three or four times, changing the pace and the inflection each time, and you will begin to see how, in two words, the Lord gave us a lifetime of work—of purposeful, godly living. "DO GOOD!"

And then, by assuming God's work as our work, we will "settle in the land" (Ps. 37:3), the "farm" He gave us, and "find safe pasture": security, sustenance, and serenity. That's really living! Try it and teach it.

11

Big as the World

Scripture: Ecclesiastes 11:7—12:14

> ". . . *The use of books is endless, and much study is wearisome" (Eccles. 12:12, NEB).*

It is clear from this scriptural reference that excessive devotion to books brings weariness. But if we read on only one more verse we will discover that relating our studies to the fear of God brings them out of the wearisome stage.

Exactly how can this be done? I am steadily working on answers to this question. I can suggest to you only a thought or two. When you reflect on these ideas and begin to teach accordingly, you will find that one idea breeds many more.

First then, begin to think of "the fear of the Lord" in elementary, down-to-earth ways. One way in which we can show that we "fear God"—that we "think the world and all of Him"—is to know more of God's world. If "the earth is the Lord's and all that is in it", then in order to honor God, we need to know the earth, what there is in it, and what's going on in the world.

We sing "This is my Father's world," and that truth is rightfully a wonderful comfort. It ought also to be a furious spark that ignites our whole being and sets us on fire to plant His claim stakes on it.

How do we proceed in such ventures? At a testimonial Father's Day service, a child said, "I like my daddy because he takes me places." Teachers, too, ought to take their students places—explore the world with them. Such exploration need not be a physical transportation, but it ought to be a real experience, nonetheless. And studies will come to life—they will be life itself!

12

Count Your Days

Scripture: Psalm 90:12-17; Psalm 86:10-12

"Teach us to number our days . . ." (Ps. 90:12, RSV).
"Teach us to order our days rightly . . ." (Ps. 90:12, NEB).

Have you ever wondered just how long you're going to live? Well, I can tell you. According to recent charts, your life expectancy is two-thirds of the time between your present age and eighty. Let's say you're thirty. Two-thirds of fifty (the difference between eighty and thirty) is thirty-four. So, acccording to these charts, you can expect to live until you're sixty-four. Startling, isn't it?

We know, of course, that this calculation is only an expectancy, not a guarantee. But it does make us stop to think seriously about "counting our days" to make our days count ("to order our days rightly"). And the psalmist tells us that for such daily wisdom we need divine instruction.

> Teach me, O Lord, Thy holy way,
> And give me an obedient mind;
> That in Thy service I may find
> My soul's delight from day to day.
>
> Help me, O Saviour, here to trace
> The sacred footsteps Thou hast trod;
> And, meekly walking with my God,
> To grow in goodness, truth, and grace.
>
> William T. Matson

Suggestion: Prayerfully plan your life again today, and work out your plan, allowing for interruptions as God-sent opportunities for service.

13

Get Your Sleep!

Scripture: Psalm 127

> ". . . *for He gives to his beloved sleep*" (Ps. 127:2, RSV).
> (*marginal reading:* "*giveth* in *sleep*")
> ". . . *my sleep was pleasant to me*" (Jer. 31:26, RSV).

Last night I went to bed too tired to think. It had been "one of those days"—a barrage of questions, of tensions, of over-taxation. But the Lord gave me the strength to carry on and the wisdom to meet each situation as it arose. Then as I grew weary toward the end of the day, He commanded me to put all books and papers aside and to go to bed on time. I did. My only prayer was, "Dear Lord, You know all about it. You also know me and You know how much I need You. You're my commander-in-chief and You're in full command. Take over, Lord."

And He did. This morning I woke up singing. I could hardly believe it, but it was real. The first thought that came to me was the words of the old, beautiful hymn:

> My faith looks up to Thee,
> Thou Lamb of Calvary, Savior divine. . . .

It was a beautiful, a delicious experience. I discovered anew that the Lord not only "gives His beloved sleep" but He gives to them "*in* sleep." *In* sleep my whole being was renewed; I received new faith, restored energy, and fresh grace.

Thank You, Lord, for putting me to sleep and giving to me in sleep what I need for today, just as You said You would. .

I have often told prospective teachers and teachers in the field every day, "Get your sleep! Tired teachers cheat children."

And now I would add, "Tired people cheat God. Those who drive themselves too much and deprive themselves of sleep rob God of His way to revive them. So, get your sleep. It's part of God's prescription for productive living and rousing teaching.

14

Blest!

Scripture: Psalm 1

"Blessed is the man . . ." (Ps. 1:1a, RSV).

Excitement was in the air yesterday. The names of those chosen for the varsity squad had been posted, and "the chosen" were jubilant. That reminded me of many similar occasions for celebration—honor rolls, music or drama performing groups, and contest winners.

Teachers rejoice with their students in their successes but often find it hard to say for themselves amid the many pressures of everyday activities, "Thank God, I too have been chosen. I am really blessed!"

Blessed! That's the key word. It's not that I did something so great, but God did great things for me and will do great things through me. God chose me for His team, and I am confident He's going to make a beautiful player out of me. The training will be rigorous, but my coach is my God. And I trust Him. He's great! I am blessed!

> His goodness to me, His blessing so free,
> I could not repay if I lived eternally;
> So, I will use the life that He gives
> To tell the world of His goodness to me.
> Lewis Erwin

Recommended "conditioning" exercise: Read five or ten psalms today and underscore all the references to *bless, blessing,* and *blessed.* Then, note the conditions for blessedness, and you will develop real muscle.

15

How Blest!

Scripture: Matthew 5:1-10

"How blest are those who show mercy;
mercy shall be shown to them" (Matt. 5:7, NEB).

Tim came to me last week in desperation. He needed help in planning a rather difficult project. He had gone from one teacher to another and several had given him suggestions, but no one felt he had the time or the competence to give the young man the direction he needed. And I must confess that I did not feel equal to the task. But something told me (the Holy Spirit, I trust) that I could not send this needy person on his way and feel justified. So, I prayed briefly before the time of our conference together: "Lord, help me to help Tim." We then spent a pleasant forty-five minutes together, developed an initial plan, and set up another appointment time.

That was last week. Meanwhile he gave me his first draft so that I could be ready for our next session. But yesterday I was sick and just had to lie back and forget about books and papers for a day.

Today Tim met me between classes and said, "Shall I still come in tomorrow at 2:30?"

And I said, "Yes, I'll try to read your paper tonight so that I'll be ready for you."

Then he looked at me a moment and said, "I know you were sick yesterday and I think I'd be demanding too much of you to take another hour of your time tomorrow. I can wait until next week."

Dear God, You are amazing! You gave me the grace to show mercy to Tim in his distress last week. Now You used him to relieve my load and demonstrate Your mercy today. How blest I am! And I'm sure Tim will be blessed, too. It's just as You said: Mercy breeds mercy. Help me to be an instrument of Your mercy and then to see its rewards.

16

We "Beasties"

Scripture: Psalm 73

"When my soul was embittered. . . .
I was like a beast toward thee" (Ps. 73:21a, 22b, RSV).

Like a beast! When have I ever acted like a beast? I'm not a sexual pervert. I'm reasonably well controlled. I'm not running wild. What is the bestial behavior of which the psalmist speaks?

He gives us the clue in describing his conflict in vv. 3, 5. "For I was envious of the arrogant, when I saw the prosperity of the wicked. . . . They are not in trouble as other men are. . . ." "For all the day long I have been stricken, and chastened every morning" (v. 14).

What's the use? I can't help being bitter, Lord. I work diligently and conscientiously but there are so many obstacles every day, so many headaches. I'm knocking myself out, Lord, and very few seem to notice. At times not even You seem to care. Sometimes I wonder whether You are really there.

Oh, God, what did I say? I'm so bitter I act like a beast. Beasts respond to stimuli without any thought. They follow a simple stimulus-response pattern. They feel the prick of a stick, and they kick back. So often I do the same. Trouble strikes and I turn sour on life. I indulge in self-pity, bitterness, and backbiting.

Thank you, Lord, for bringing me to my senses, for helping me to see that I am not a beast but a redeemed human being, a person for whom You gave Your life and to whom You gave the Spirit so that I might live—live abundantly and cheerfully and triumphantly. Thanks for noticing my tears and for putting a song back into my life.

> Though flesh and heart should faint and fail,
> The Lord will ever be
> The strength and portion of my heart,
> My God eternally.

William U. Butcher

31

17

As a Weaned Child

Scripture: Psalm 131

> *"I do not busy myself with . . . things too marvellous for me. No; I submit myself . . . as a weaned child clinging to its mother"* *(Ps. 131:1, NEB).*

Why is one of our most promising students now afflicted with a deadly disease? Why were both parents of four young children suddenly taken from them in a horrible car accident today?

Questions, frustrations, anxieties often flood our souls. How can we cope with these perplexities and help children to handle some of the "unanswerables" in life?

Time and again I have come back to Psalm 131 and found a resting place there for my troubled mind. And I sing it as I learned it early in life in the metrical version:

> I do not seek to know the things God's wisdom has
> denied.
> With childlike trust, O Lord, in Thee I calmly rest,
> Contented as a little (weaned) child upon his
> mother's breast.
>
> Robert Jackson

The figure of a weaned child is a beautiful one. A weaned child is a very frustrated person. He cannot understand why his mother no longer feeds him. But he can find rest because his mother still holds him.

Take the sweet old Swedish hymn which sums it all up, and make it a part of your being and of those entrusted to you:

> Children of the heavenly Father
> Safely to His bosom gather.
> Nestling bird nor star of heaven
> Such a refuge e'er was given.
>
> Though He giveth or He taketh,
> God His children ne'er forsaketh
> His the loving purpose solely
> To preserve them pure and holy.
>
> Carolina Sandell Berg

18

Like a Marathon Runner

Scripture: Hebrews 12, Philippians 3

". . . one thing I do . . . I press on . . ." (Phil. 3:13b, 14a, RSV).

> I'm pressing on the upward way;
> New heights I'm gaining every day.
> Still praying as I onward bound,
> "Lord, plant my feet on higher ground."

This was the favorite song of Miss Johanna Veenstra, a stalwart pioneer missionary in Nigeria. The above text from Philippians was used by a dear missionary cousin of mine in her ringing farewell address some years ago. And now today, more than ever before, I catch the message of the above text and the vision of the above-mentioned missionaries and Kingdom workers of all times and places. I realize this morning in more ways than I can tell you that I, too, am running a marathon race, and I want more than anything else to reach that finish line and hear the Lord of my life—my God, my Savior, my King—say just three words to me, "Well done, Nelle."

And you, teachers everywhere, need to know that your task is just as great a mission as any other assignment in the Kingdom of God and that it is a race, not a "rat-race," but a race of the highest order—an athletic course in God's school from start to finish. I trust you can say that you are in this race for God, that you are drawing on His strength daily, and that you are exerting yourself fully, gladly, and perserveringly to realize God's goals in your classroom and in every arena of life.

So then, "run, man, run!" and sing as you go: "I'm pressing on. . . ." But also add (and take time to think about what you are saying):

> Lead on, O King eternal,
> The day of march has come. . . .

19

When Fear Cramps Your Heart

Scripture: Isaiah 42:1-13; 43:1-5a; John 14

> *". . . Have no fear; for I have paid your ransom; I have called you by name and you are my own" (Isa. 43:1b, NEB).*
>
> *"Have no fear; for I am with you . . ." (Isa. 43:5a, NEB).*

One of my favorite bits of poetic prose was written by Philip Booth after trying to teach one of his young daughters how to swim, specifically, how to float. I'm sure he intended to have her read it at different points in her life. I keep coming back to it and marvel at the beautiful wisdom and comfort expressed in these words:

First Lesson

Lie back, daughter, let your head be tipped back in the cup of my hand. Gently, and I will hold you. Spread your arms wide, lie out on the stream and look high at the gulls. A deadman's float is face down. You will dive and swim soon enough where this tidewater ebbs to the sea. Daughter, believe me, when you tire on the long thrash to your island, lie up, and survive. As you float now, where I held you and let go, remember when fear cramps your heart what I told you: lie gently and wide to the light-year stars, lie back, and the sea will hold you.

We all have times "when fear cramps our hearts." There are times of illness, of financial stress, of anxiety about our work and our future, tensions without and conflicts within. But always the Lord speaks like the father quoted above; yet with even more certainty, with unfailing assurance, "Lie back, my child, and *I* will hold you."

And when we lie back, we will see the carefree birds and the steady-shining stars. But more than that, we will see the face of our God and hear Him say to us, " (Name), you are precious to me . . . I gave my life for you . . . I love you (Isa. 43:4). Don't be afraid. I'm holding you. And 'what my hand holds, none can snatch away.' " (Isa. 43:13b).

20
Prayer and Purpose

Scripture: Psalm 67

> *". . . God make his face shine upon us, that his ways may be known on earth. . . ."*
> *"God grant us his blessing, that all the ends of the earth may fear him" (Ps. 67:1, 2, 7, NEB).*

What a stir we had throughout our land when prayer in public schools was outlawed! The matter is still a live issue in many parts of our country. Often we hear it said that such a ruling is powerful evidence of the spiritual degeneration of our nation. Perhaps it is.

We ought not deceive ourselves, however, to think that every request for God's blessing, just any kind of prayer, is pleasing to God. Many prayers are not prayers at all but a form of religious calisthenic or tonic. They make us feel better. But prayer to God without strict attention to God's purposes is an offense to God. God outlawed purposeless prayers ages ago.

The psalmist in the above passage clearly associates prayer with purpose. "God bless us *that his ways may be known.*" The implication is clear: we have no right to ask God for a blessing unless it is for such a purpose. We may not pray unless we have some intention of relating our requests to our lives, of somehow making God's ways better known.

Sometimes I am expected to lead in prayer several times a day, and I know some of you are, too. I find that determining my purpose for the class or the occasion sharpens my focus in prayer and delivers me from "vain repetitions." When I know how I intend to carry out God's purpose in a given situation, I find new delight in prayer and new assurance of His blessing. For God is faithful, and when we come to Him, saying, "Help me, God, to teach this class or perform this work so that others may sense beyond a doubt that You are here," then "God, our God, *will* bless us" (Ps. 67:6). How? By giving us new insight into His ways and zest for purposeful prayer.

21

Tell Them the Story

Scripture: Deuteronomy 6:4-9, 20-25; Joshua 4:1-7; Psalm 78; 105; 106; Matthew 5-7; Matthew 13

> *"And these words . . . you shall talk of . . . when you sit . . . and when you walk . . ." (Deut. 6:6-7, RSV).*

I don't know how often you take time to read the Scriptures recommended on these pages. If you do, you will have a week of revitalizing reading in the above passages and a lifetime of work—of wonderful, life-giving work. Take a good dose of Life so that this Life lives in you and is yours to give.

How shall you give it? *Tell it.* We often sing, "I love to *tell* the story. . . ." and then we sit down and *read* it. There is a legitimate place for reading, to be sure, but the most basic and still the most effective way is *telling.* It is the way Moses and Joshua prescribed for the education of the children of Israel, the way the psalmist recommends for people of all ages, and the way Jesus taught. On the basis of these models from the Scriptures, I believe we need to do more story-*telling* in teaching.

My position has become more like a conviction in recent years as I observe the current trends in Bible teaching and note teachers' (parents', too) dependence on materials. At a recent seminar for training nationals to teach their people with their own resources, I learned a lot from Gus, a Liberian master teacher. He testified that the most efficient and effective means of getting the gospel to the masses in his land was to use native, natural story-tellers. And as the man talked about his program for training such people, I wanted to shout: "Cheers for Gus! You've got it, man!"

Tell the story! Tell the children the glorious works of God "so that they may set their hope in God" (Ps. 78:4b, 7a, RSV).

22

Shake Hands

Scripture: II Corinthians 13

> *"Thou dost hold my right hand" (Ps. 73:23b, RSV).*
> *"Thy right hand is my support" (Ps. 63:8b, NEB).*
> *"Do you not realize that Jesus Christ is in you?" (II Cor. 13:5, RSV).*

My friend Ray and I don't sit and chat, but whenever we meet, however brief the exchange, we have fun. He's a bright ray (pun intended). I don't see him very often at church. He says he's usually out preaching, and I suppose I better believe him. But last Sunday morning he was standing near the doorway as church was dismissed. He greeted me warmly with a handshake. I quipped, "You must have been reading Phillips lately, Ray. He (Phillips) translates the passage, 'Greet one another with a holy kiss' into 'a handshake all around . . .' " (II Cor. 13:12).

To that Ray retorted with an affected but effective seriousness, "That sounds like a watered-down version to me."

That retort sparked me to reply with a quizzical look and tone, "Is that what you call 'tongue in cheek' humor?" And for once —just once—Ray had no reply. I felt so good and smug.

But throughout the week I thought about the matter of greeting and the wordless ways of expressing warmth and concern recommended in the Bible. Then one day during that same week a young father shared with me some of the questions his four-year-old son asks him about God. The child wants to know for instance, "How can I know that God is real, that He is really here with me when I can't see Him?" I don't pretend to have the best and fullest answer to that question, but I believe on the basis of such Scriptural references as quoted above that the Lord has given us ways to demonstrate, concretely show, His love and the reality of His steady support. One way is to use our hands, to reach out and clasp someone else's hand.

So many, oh, so many of our students, colleagues, friends —people all around us—are seeking encouragement and assurance. In the past five years I have listened to so many people as they revealed their heartaches and struggles. And I have struggled to know how to help them. In answer to my daily prayer: "Spirit of God, my teacher be, showing the things of Christ to me," the Lord has shown me one thing about hands that may be of help to you.

When someone has revealed his problem to me and together we have discussed ways to handle it, I often take his hand just as he is leaving my office and say, "Do you feel my hand in yours? I can reach out my hand to you only because God gives me the strength and the desire to do so. And even more amazing to me and yet because God says it, I know it's true, *my hand is God's hand.* God has no hands on earth but the hands of His people. And just as sure (and even more so) as you feel my hand, you can know that God has taken hold of your hand. And God does not let go. Believe it! Put one hand in God's hand, use the other one to reach out to others, and you will be a new person. You will live a new life, and you will sing anew.

Again I say, use your hands to demonstrate to children of all ages that God is real, that God is love, and that God holds on.

23

Studied Communication

Scripture: Colossians 4:5-6; Proverbs 12:15-23

> *"Study how best to talk with each person you meet"* (Col 4:6b, NEB).
> *"The tongue of the wise heals"* (Prov. 12:18b, NEB).

Our annual literary magazine is just out. In it is a poem by one of my colleagues that prompted me to do some soul-searching and to observe interpersonal relationships more insightfully. Here it is:

Community

Studied separateness.
Why it infected the bone
Is anyone's guess.

We sought loneliness
And, talking only by phone,
Studied separateness.

What crowded room's press
First turned greeting eyes to stone
Is anyone's guess.

What seemed haughtiness
Was perhaps merely full-blown
Studied separateness.

Whether to impress
Or just to be left alone
Is anyone's guess.

Why we became less
Hopeful and, loath to be known,
Studied separateness
Is anyone's guess.

Nick Barker

I was struck by the truth in this piece. Studied separateness. I wonder what would happen in schools, churches, and all Christian communities if we took the Bible seriously and practiced studied communication. It seems to me that that is exactly what Paul is recommending to the Colossians when he says, *"Study* how best to talk with each person you meet" (Col. 4:6b, NEB).

What would such studied communication require? It would certainly require time, prayerful deliberation, keen sensitivity to the needs of others, and a generous, gentle spirit such as Christ showed to the woman at the well. And such communication would require the highest motivation—*healing* (salvation means healing, you know).

Yes, I just wonder what would happen if we substituted "studied communication" for "studied separateness."

Recommended exercise: Keep a brief anecdotal record of your conversations for the next two days. Adopt as your slogan the words from Proverbs: "The tongue of the wise heals." Check yourself out at the end of two days. Did your tongue work right?

> How good and pleasant is the sight
> When brethren make it their delight
> To dwell in blest accord;
> The Lord *commands* His blessing there,
> And they that walk in love shall share
> In life that never ends.
>
> (Ps. 133, metrical version, emphasis added)

24

Deal Gently

Scripture: Isaiah 61:1-3

"The Lord God has given me the tongue of a teacher and skill to console the weary" (Isa. 50:4a, NEB).
"Restore . . . in a spirit of gentleness" (Gal. 6:1b, RSV).
"Bear one another's burdens, and so fulfil the law of Christ" (Gal. 6:2a, RSV).

"Spring is bursting out all over" these days. The trees, the flowers, the birds—"all nature sings."

While riding through a delightful woodland yesterday, I noticed a delicate anemone just beginning to bloom. I recalled a quotation that has stuck with me though I have long forgotten the author. He said, "Remember a writer is an anemone, and an anemone is a tender plant." The article in which I read that quote said that a certain editor had that saying on his desk to remind him how to deal with manuscripts.

I am sure that many teachers often feel, too, that they are dealing with anemones, tender plants. We have but to recall the many times that a student has handed to us one of his first efforts in writing some special private piece. He would like to have someone he trusts read it and tell him what to do with the piece and how to go on toward further productivity. At the same time he is afraid of being hurt or even crushed. So, he submits his work quietly but entreatingly, "Deal gently. This piece may not be great art, but it is part of me. Preserve me but help me to be even more." And it is agonizingly difficult at times to do just that in teaching—to preserve the person and help him. It's fairly easy to say what *not* to do. It's hard to tell students (or anyone, in fact) what *to* do—"in a spirit of gentleness" (Gal. 6:1). It takes special eyes to see the tenderness of the plant and the buds of potential blossom in it. Then, it takes a special touch, gentle hands, to sustain the plant and to cultivate its growth. The Lord Jesus gave us many models for such teaching. I enjoy searching them out and seeking ways to use them for my own teaching.

A sixteen-year-old boy wrote these words of dedication on his first "volume" of his own poetry:

> *To my English teacher*
> *who saw the tiny flecks of gold*
> *in my tons of ore*
> *and helped me pan them.*

Flecks, tons, panning—all part of golden days in teaching. Don't you envy just a bit the teacher who received such a tribute?

Recommended reading: Read one chapter a day in an old, but timeless, book, *The Great Physician,* by the master British teacher-preacher, G. Campbell Morgan. That book about Christ's teaching ministry is one of the best courses in "sensitivity training" and "individualized instruction" that I have ever read.

25

Get Tough

Scripture: Galatians 2:11-21; Galatians 6:1-5

> ". . . I opposed him [Peter] to his face, because he stood
> condemned" (Gal. 2:11b, RSV).
> "For each man will have to bear his own load" (Gal. 6:5,
> RSV).

For years I have wrestled with the first five verses of Galatians
6. In a very short space, Paul says at one point: "Bear one
another's burdens. . . ," and then a little further along he says
with a startling directness: "Each man will have to bear his own
load."

Throughout my teaching I've been more or less aware (more at
some times than at others) of the need to help students bear their
burdens. The force of the need at other times to help students
bear their own load of responsibility hit me hard last week.
Because of my lack of discernment in knowing when to "deal
gently" and when to "get tough," I missed an opportunity to
teach a young man a much-needed lesson in assuming responsibility himself for the work at hand. (And I'm still irritated with
myself because I can "get tough." Twenty years of teaching in
junior high school helped me develop that kind of muscle.) But,
as I said, on this occasion I "goofed." I restrained myself, rather
quietly backed away from the issue when I should have tackled
the problem right then and there and corrected the young man,
who needed correction rather than my restraint.

Dave (not real name) came to me with his reading record,
submitted late without a good reason for doing so. At the same
time he passed along two suggestions for improving the course.
Now, usually I accept suggestions from students with real appreciation because I recognize them as fellow-teachers in a
sense. Daily I learn from my students. In this case, however, I
resented the suggestions, especially the one about having addi-

tional class sessions, loosely organized, small group meetings to discuss the "philosophical implications of children's literature." I resented the suggestion because I already have more work than I can handle and especially because the person making the suggestion has missed more regular class sessions than anyone else (fifty-eight students in the class). Furthermore, when he does please to come to class, he rarely, if ever, contributes a word. And when he came around with his suggestions, I should have "opposed him to the face" as Paul once did to Peter and used that time to show him his need "to bear his own load" responsibly and faithfully.

O Lord, give me discernment so that I may know in my teaching every day when to apply balm and when to use the surgeon's knife and thus exercise a real healing ministry—a ministry like that of the Master Teacher.

Postscript: There is a sequel to this account.

Dave met me as I was enroute to the last session of the class. He tried to give me more smooth talk, hand me his last project, and then skip class. God gave me the strength to accept no excuses, to tell Dave his fault, and to insist on his attending that last class. Dave was speechless and angry. He struggled with himself for the first half hour of the class. But, toward the end, his expression changed, and he asked for an opportunity to share his project. He had an artistic piece of work and presented it masterfully. After class, he thanked me heartily for not letting him "get by with it."

I thanked God for giving me a second chance to help Dave "bear his own load."

26

Teaching Is a Two-Way Street

Scripture: Ecclesiastes 11:1-7

> *"Cast your bread upon the waters, for you will find it after many days" (Eccles. 11:1, RSV).*
> *"In the morning sow your seed, and at evening withhold not your hand" (Eccles. 11:6a, RSV).*

I learn from my students every day. I have told many of my friends, both students and colleagues, this truth; and have "preached" it to many groups in conventions or similar gatherings. The reinforcement of this truth has been coming to me in overwhelming ways during the closing weeks of this semester. I can only begin to tell in what ways and to what extent my students have taught me. I share with you the following bit of verse that came to me from a student in a children's literature class last week. It is just one specific way in which students teach teachers. I know it will illuminate life for you and make you more keenly aware of some of the best resources at your command and close at hand—your own students.

Poetic Bits for the Teacher

LAZY ONE
> You never had your homework done;
> You never joined in group sports.
> How were we to know you were physically ill?

SHY GIRL, SHY BOY
> You sat in your corner quiet as a mouse!
> Why did we sit by not knowing or caring that
> you did not understand?

SLEEPY ONE
> You slept day in and day out
> Not knowing the world around you
> was moving on without you. How
> could we know you slept because you
> could not face life?

LOUD ONE

       Your voice being heard by all,
       All the turmoil and the fights you caused;
       How could we know you were really sad
       and looking for love?

PRETTY ONE

       How we admired your blue eyes
       and golden locks, forgetting
       the real inside and teaching
       you the hardships of life.

DILIGENT ONE

       You struggled day by day, but you excelled in
       learning more than you were asked.
       Where have we failed you? Was it
       not knowing you were lonely and
       were fighting to survive?

UGLY ONE

       We tossed you aside not recognizing
       your true beauty and helping you
       to make it show.

Mary Ellen Payne

27

The Four Tests of Wisdom

*"If any of you lacks wisdom, let him ask God . . .
and it will be given him" (James 1:5, RSV).
"But the wisdom from above is in the first place
pure; and then peace-loving, considerate, and open
to reason" (James 3:17a, NEB).*

Often I have read the first text from James and tried to practice it. Only recently did I discover the nature of "the wisdom that is from above."

I can tell you what prompted my discovery. I had to meet with one of my colleagues over a rather delicate issue. The situation was very tense, and I felt I desperately needed special grace and wisdom. So I began reading the Book of James because I recalled that familiar text about asking for wisdom. But this time I just kept on reading, and then, suddenly I came upon the words in James 3:17.

It was a wonderful experience. I wondered why I had missed seeing that passage all these years and yet rejoiced that I found it now when I so much needed it.

I checked myself out before approaching my colleague on the delicate issue between us and before us. Let's see: "The wisdom that is from above is first *pure.*" I thought, "Well, I'm not tackling this problem for any selfish gain to be sure. So I guess I pass that test." I looked at the next: "peace-loving." And I thought, "That's exactly what I'm trying to do in this case. If ever I was pursuing (chasing after) peace, it is in this particular instance." What's the third test? "Considerate." I reflected upon that and could say, "Yes, I want to give the person all due consideration. God knows I want to be a healing agent in this case." And then: "open to reason." "Oh, thank God," I said, "He has given me that grace, too, for this time. I am most willing to listen to the other person concerned." After that kind of checking on myself, I could approach the person and the problem thankfully and calmly.

Thanks, Lord, for such provision. Once again You proved to

me that You will do just what You say. All we have to do is *ask*, *seek*, and then expect You to reply. How invigorating is Your wisdom! How deadly is our folly, for it is as the psalmist said, "If he be not truly wise, man is like the beast that dies" (Ps. 49:20).

Recommended exercise for developing wisdom and beautifying interpersonal relationships:

Read Proverbs 10-24, underscoring as you read the many references to wisdom in speech and its effect upon human relationships. Here is a beginning:

"There is no spite in a just man's talk" (Prov. 10:18a, NEB).

"When men talk too much, sin is never far away;
common sense holds its tongue" (Prov. 10:19, NEB).

"A soothing word is a staff of life, but a mis-
chievous tongue breaks the spirit" (Prov. 15:4, NEB).

"A man may be pleased with his own retort;
how much better is a word in season!" (Prov. 15:23, NEB).

28

Who Will Teach Helen?

Scripture: Psalm 139

"Thou it was who didst fashion my inward parts . . . I will praise thee, for thou dost fill me with awe; wonderful thou art, and wonderful thy works" (Ps. 139: 13-14, NEB)

A beginning teacher came to me for counsel. She asked me to visit her classes and help her to be more effective. She felt she was failing.

When she came to see me at the end of the observations, I really didn't know what to say. I listened hard and prayed much as she poured out her feelings of inadequacy. She asked for specific suggestions to improve her teaching.

As I looked at her bent shoulders and anxious face, the above words from Psalm 139 came to my mind. I felt I had to give Helen a new appreciation for who she was—a person "fearfully and wonderfully made"—before I could say anything about how she performed. A wild idea hit me. I told her, "Helen, I'm going to prescribe an exercise for you. Practice it every night for a week. Go dancing around your apartment, fling your arms around freely, and say aloud: "Praise the Lord, I am a person, created by the Almighty God, redeemed by the Lord Jesus Christ, endowed by the Holy Spirit, and commissioned to teach. Praise the Lord, I am Helen Ray!" Then look at yourself in a mirror and say, "God made me beautiful."

Helen left smiling. But she could not carry out the exercise and express praise for her person. She failed in teaching. But who failed to teach Helen?

29

A Cheerful Face

Scripture: Proverbs 15:13-15

"A merry heart makes a cheerful face" (Prov. 15:13a, NEB).

A popular national educator, Ole Sands, once said, "Too many teachers look as if they were weaned on a pickle!" I read that line, rushed to a mirror, took a good look, and said, "Oh, horrors, it's true!"

A cheerful face—we all recognize it as a strong asset in teaching. (Somewhere I heard recently that 53 percent of effective communication is facial expression.) We all relish cheerfulness and a happy look, but how do we get it? Is it a matter of autosuggestion—of saying to oneself, "I ought to smile more; so I will." Such a practice may produce more smiles for a time, but the procedure is too artificial to last.

The writer of Proverbs associates a cheerful face with a merry heart. Then he suggests that the health of our whole being (heart and countenance) is closely related to our speech. "Pleasant words are . . . sweetness to the soul and health to the body" (Prov. 16:24, RSV).

Words can produce merry hearts and cheerful faces.

Prescription: Read Proverbs 15, 16, and 17 and note all the references to speech or the use of language—words, tongue, mouth, lips, etc. Apply the prescription as directed for two weeks. If no change occurs, double the dosage and add chapter 18 of Proverbs. Do *not* keep this medicine away from children.

30

Laughter

Scripture: Psalm 126 and 103

"Then our mouth was filled with laughter . . ." (Ps. 126:2a, RSV).

One of my friends, a former student, is a "bubbler," and when we get together, we have so much fun. We provoke one another to laughter. She called me long distance yesterday to discuss one of her projects, but even in that process, we laughed so much more than we talked. And I felt so delightfully refreshed.

Laughter—what a gift! And what a joyous quality to have and to cultivate!

How can we have it, exercise it, and help others to use it as an instrument of praise? The writer of Psalm 126 tells us that by looking back and by looking ahead, we can be "filled with laughter" now. The secret is in knowing what to look for. In looking back, we note: "The Lord has done great things for us . . ." (Ps. 126:3a, RSV). ". . . Forget none of His benefits" (Ps. 103:2b, NEB). In looking ahead, we know: "The Lord's love never fails . . ." (Ps. 103:17, NEB) and we shall "reap with shouts of joy!" (Ps. 126:5b, RSV).

So, because we have experienced God's gracious love in the past and know by faith in His word that we can trust Him for the future, we have hope and joy in the present.

Then, laugh!

And sing:

> Let us be joyful, we that are Christian;
> Lift heart and voice in jubilant song.
> So many reasons have we for gladness
> We should be singing all the day long.

31

Rainy Days

Scripture: Psalm 65; Deuteronomy 32:2-3

"Thou visitest the land and waterest it. Thou greatly enrichest it; God's river is brimful of water.
Thou providest them grain, for so Thou hast ordained it; watering the furrows, softening its ridges,
Thou makest it soft with showers; Thou dost bless its vegetation" (Ps. 65:9-10, Berkeley).

Had we only sunshine all the year around
Without the blessing of refreshing rain,
Should we scatter seeds upon the fallow ground
And hope to gather flowers, fruit, and grain?

Sunshine and rain, refreshing, reviving rain,
Light of truth and love, showers from above,
Sunshine and rain to nourish the growing grain,
Send us, Lord, the sunshine and the rain.

This is a song that I learned in childhood and still sing it cheerfully on rainy days. There are many other songs about rain. What is the first one that comes to your mind? (I trust you have a storehouse of songs. If not, begin building at once.)

How do you react to rain? Likely your reaction will depend on your location, your plans for the day, your reflective and imaginative powers, and a number of variables. Some of you dread rainy days because they confine you and your class. "Indoor recesses" offer no relief or release. Others of you welcome rainy days from time to time for they give you an opportunity to break loose, to change your pace, to lay aside your usual plans, and to be spontaneous and fresh.

Spontaneity, however, does not arise from a vacuum. The most creative people are very observant and have a file of resources (mental or physical). Get your idea file out and *plan a day of praise for rain*. Take a poetic bit of Scripture such as the reference from Psalm 65 quoted above and perhaps one or two more. Take time to let the beauty and the precision of the imagery really "soak in." Then think of music, songs, and poetry appropriate to the subject and to your class. Go on and dream of ways in which you can involve your class in planning a refreshing study of rain and expressions of praise about it. (Some children, and even adults, have never really *felt* rain. You may want to take a walk in the rain to get the feel, the smell, and the taste of it.)

I predict that at the end of such a day you will know more of what it means to "sing a new song to the Lord." And you will have fresh insights into the prayer of Moses (which is my motto):

> "May my teaching drop as the rain . . .
> As the gentle rain upon the tender grass"
> (Deut. 32:2, RSV).

Resources: *Let Youth Praise Him.* Grand Rapids: National Union of Christian Schools.

Joy Is Like the Rain (recording by Medical Missions Sisters).

Creative Brooding by Robert Raines. New York: Macmillan, 1970.

Let Them Write Poetry by Nina Walter. Chicago: Holt, Rinehart and Winston, 1962.

32

At the Front of the Battle

Scripture: Psalm 27, Ephesians 6:10-20

"Be strong, and let your heart take courage . . ." (Ps. 27:14b, RSV).
"Finally, be strong in the Lord and in the strength of his might" (Eph. 6:10, RSV).

For the past two days I've been singing an old song that I must have learned in early childhood. (I've looked through various hymn books and still haven't found it.) But the song keeps coming back to my mind clear and strong, and I sing with great delight:

I've enlisted for life in the army of the Lord,
Though the fight may be long and the struggle fierce and hard,
With the armor of God and the Spirit's trusty sword
At the front of the battle you will find me.

Hear the tramp, tramp, tramping of the army
Their triumph shouting, their foes they're routing.
Hear the tramp, tramp, tramping of the army
Marching on to victory.

You, too, are on the firing line every day. As I go along writing these pieces, I often say to some of my colleagues, I consider my audience to be those who are at the battlefront and need steady cheering on every day to keep their arms strong and their hearts brave. But I know that it's not my cheers that will enable you to carry on nobly and "fight the good fight." Read Psalm 27 once again, especially the first and last verses. You will note that the strength is a result of *waiting* for the Lord (waiting for orders), and courage comes from *letting* the Lord act in your life. May God help us to wait for Him and His orders before we act. "Trust in the Lord and He will act" (Ps. 37:5b, NEB). Then we will be strong and courageous. And we can be sure of being able to stand at the front of the battle if our testimony is that of the psalmist: "I believe that I shall see the goodness of the Lord in the land of the living" (Ps. 27:13).

33

Chase Out Injustice

Scripture: Mark 11:15-17; Psalm 84

"Be angry but do not sin" (Eph. 4:26a, RSV).
"Blessed are the men whose strength is in thee" (Ps. 84:5a, RSV).

How often have you been told that Christians ought never to be angry—to "get mad"? Christ Himself became angry on at least two occasions that are recorded for us in the Scriptures. On one of these occasions He was furious and really cleaned house in the temple in order to restore honesty and justice.

By so doing, He gave us a model for "cleaning house" in other areas, too, also in the educational world. Those who exercise such courage must be aware of the dangers and their own vulnerability. Yet Christ's model stands and Paul's injunction to the Ephesians is clear: "Be angry . . ." The danger comes in attacking innocent people and in exercising our anger for selfish ends. And the vulnerability is obvious: the attacker may be hurt in the process. Such hurt is revealed by the psalmist:

> I have followed truth and justice,
> Leave me not in deep distress;
> Be my help and my protection. . . .
> (metrical version of Psalm 119)

The painful alienation it may cause is expressed in one of Ibsen's plays: "Those who stand for the truth must learn to be lonely."

But "having done all," we must "stand," (Eph. 6:13) and be willing to pay the price, for God's sake, for the sake of truth and justice. Standing for the truth and seeking justice can be another way of cleansing educational institutions of certain unjust, un-Christ-like practices. When policies override people, when masterful teachers are dropped or considered less desirable for the sake of balancing budgets, then we must ask ourselves: Is this another form of making God's temple "a den of robbers"?

Some of you may be in the very position of which I speak, either as an employer or as an employee (present or prospective). All of you are in a position to observe and to promote justice in educational policies. And when there is injustice, God's people are to recognize it and fight it. Such "speaking out" is surely part of seeking first the Kingdom of God *and His righteousness.*

But remember that such seeking requires that one "deny himself, take up his cross, and follow me." The road is rough. But we have a fearless, flawless Leader, who has walked that road and opened it for us. In fact, He Himself is the Way. And He always leads. The hard part is to always let Him lead. In it all, though, He offers His company and His steadying hand as we "go from strength to strength" (Ps. 84:7a).

Read the little classic for Christian living: *Sit, Walk, Stand,* by Watchman Nee, first published in Bombay, India, in 1957. Now in its third British edition, it is distributed in America by the Christian Literature Crusade, Inc., Pennsylvania Avenue, Fort Washington, Pa.

His concluding paragraph is also an introduction to a life modeled after Christ:

> The Christian life consists of sitting with Christ, walking by Him and standing in Him. We begin our spiritual life by resting in the finished work of the Lord Jesus. That rest is the source of our strength for a consistent and unfaltering walk in the world. And at the end of a gruelling warfare . . . we are found standing with Him at last in triumphant possession of the field.

34

Sing!

Scripture: Judges 5

> ". . . to the Lord I will sing . . .
> Awake, awake, utter a song!
> (Judg. 5:3, 12a, RSV).

Thank God I was reared in an atmosphere of song! My earliest recollections are those of hearing my mother sing to me. Then I recall times of singing as a family around the piano, singing in church, singing daily in the classroom—it seems to me now that singing has always been one of the chief ingredients of my life.

God commands us to sing. (Sometimes we get and impart the impression that God's decrees for our lives are so demanding. Take a fresh look at His commands and discover how delightful they really are.) The Bible is replete with invitations to sing. Just for fun and increased joy in living, go through the Bible and read one song from it each day. You will be amazed at the variety of authors, occasions, and themes. You will be strengthened, too, in faith because of the unity that persists—the one basis for all song: the unfailing love of God.

Deborah and Barak experienced this love and led the people in song to the Mighty Conqueror. Read their song. (Judg. 5). There are many surprising lines in it. The rousing invitation for all of God's people to join in song is clear, however. The concluding line is food for reflection and strength for action: "O Lord, let all who love thee be like the sun rising in strength" (Judg. 5:31b, NEB).

Be like the sun! That's amazing! Have you seen a sunrise lately, resplendent in its display of color and promise? Breathtaking, isn't it? We're often told that we are more like the moon—a reflection of light. But here in Deborah's song we are asked to be like the sun—a source of light. And we can be such a light only because the Source is within us and causes His brightness, strength, and beauty to radiate from us.

Today enjoy the health of God's sunshine above you, around you, and within you. Then sing about it!

35

Be a Lifter

Scripture: Isaiah 33:2-6

"O Lord . . . be our arm every morning . . ." (Isa. 33:2, RSV).

One of my "cheerleaders" sent me this bit of verse a few weeks ago:

> Every morning lean thine arms awhile
> Upon the windowsill of heaven,
> And gaze upon the Lord.
> Then, with that vision in thy heart,
> Turn strong to meet the day.

All the steps are very important. We need the leaning, but we cannot stop there. (I sometimes feel that we linger on the windowsills because I hear the song "Leaning on the everlasting arms" more than I do "Awake, my soul, stretch every nerve, and press with vigor on.") But do *lean, gaze,* then get to *work* with renewed vision and strength. *"Turn strong."*

Someone put it this way: "Be a lifter, not a leaner . . . There is only one lifter to twenty who lean." It is really not a point of "either . . . or" but another instance of "both . . . and."

Sing:

> Refresh Thy people on their toilsome way;
> Lead us from night to never-ending day. . . .
> Be Thou our Ruler, Guardian, Guide, and Stay;
> Thy Word our law, Thy paths our chosen way.
> Daniel C. Roberts

Recommended "weight-lifting" practice:

Take that song, note each noun in the request—Ruler, Guardian, Guide, Stay—and list the ways in which you would like the Lord to rule, guard, guide, and stay (support and keep) you. With such specifics for Christian living in your mind, enter your classroom. And you will see how God's arm is really and simply your own arm—how, while leaning on God, you gain the power and the joy of lifting.

36

Like a Tree Planted by the River

Scripture: Psalm 1

"He is like a tree planted by streams of water" (Ps. 1:3a, RSV).

> Glory, hallelujah!
> I shall not be moved!
> Anchored in Jehovah,
> I shall not be moved . . .
> I'm like a tree planted by the water;
> I shall not be moved!

Read Psalm 1 and memorize the third stanza (or verse); then, if at all possible, walk to a stream and find a tree. (If not possible, close your eyes and picture such a scene). When you've found a good strong tree right at the water's edge, take a long look, and think! Just think "If I love to be in God's company and eat heartily of His food, *I am like that tree.*" And you will find yourself singing, just as I am this morning as I sit looking at a sturdy sycamore tree—firmly planted, deeply rooted, unmoved by the rushing stream.

Then, as you go on thinking, you will begin to wonder, "How did that tree get to be that way?" If you reread Psalm 1 at this point, you will discover the wonderful truth (secret): God's children are planted by God Himself by God's stream. All we have to do is "lap it up"—drink and drink of the "living water" with eagerness and delight. ("His delight is in the law of the Lord," Ps. 1:2a.)

And should the stream along which our tree is planted sometimes become torrential, and even reach flood stage, may God help us to stand firm and remember that He uses stormy waters to give us deeper roots, greener leaves, and lush fruit.

> That man is nourished like a tree
> Set by the river's side:
> Its leaf is green, its fruit is sure,
> And thus his works abide.
>
> Ps. 1:3 (metrical version)

59

37

Thirsty as a Deer

Scripture: Psalm 42, Psalm 63, Isaiah 55

> *"As a deer pants for water brooks so my soul longs for Thee, O God"* (Ps. 42:1, Berkeley).
>
> *"With my whole being I thirst for God, the living God"* (Ps. 42:2a, NEB).
>
> *"O God, thou art my God, I seek thee early with a heart that thirsts for thee"* (Ps. 63:1a, NEB).

Stress is common to all of us in everyday life. The *distress* of thirst—a panting, longing thirst—is not so common, at least not an everyday experience for most of us. Yet the Bible is replete with references to thirst. In fact, it seems that only the thirsty ones are invited to "come to the waters" (Isa. 55:1) and only those who thirst for righteousness (to be made right with God and to do what is right) shall be blessed and satisfied (Matt. 5:6).

How and when do we become thirsty? The psalmist gives us the figure of a deer to help us answer this question. A deer runs, often for long distances, especially when he is being chased by hunters. A deer lives in the wilds, off the beaten path, where the streams or water holes are hard to find.

Why am I not more thirsty, Lord, or thirsty more often? Can it be that I am not aware of being hunted and thus not running from that which could take the life out of me? Have I not yet discovered how arid the world around me is, that "I wander in a desert land where all the streams are dry"? Am I deceiving myself and often imbibing so much "soft drink" that I have little thirst for the "streams of living water"?

O God, give me the insight and the courage of the psalmist and the prophets to come to You and say: Yes, Lord, that's me. That's me. Help me to see more fully how I deceive myself and to sense real thirst. O God, give me a drink so that I may sing with unfaltering voice:

> See the streams of living waters,
> Springing from eternal love,
> Well supply thy sons and daughters

And all fear of want remove:
Who can faint when such a river
Ever flows their thirst t'assuage?
Grace which like the Lord, the Giver,
Never fails from age to age.
Savior, if of Zion's city
I, through grace, a member am,
Let the world deride or pity,
I will glory in Thy name.
Fading is the worldling's pleasure,
All his boasted pomp and show;
Solid joys and lasting treasures
None but Zion's children know.

John Newton

For your planning: How will you make your students thirsty for the right things today and then what will you give them to drink? What are the "solid joys and lasting treasures"? How can they best be known and become the most vital part of teaching and living?

38

God Saves Our Tears

Scripture: Exod. 25:31-40; Ps. 56

> *"Make me a sanctuary, and I will dwell among them. Make it exactly according to the design I show you"* *(Exod. 25:8-9a, NEB).*
>
> *"Make a lampstand of pure gold"* *(Exod. 25:31a, NEB).*
>
> *"Its tongs [snuffers] and firepans [trays] shall be of pure gold"* *(Exod. 25:38a, NEB).*
>
> *"Put thou my tears in thy bottle!"* *(Ps. 56:8b, RSV).*
>
> *"Store every tear in thy flask"* *(Ps. 56:8b, NEB).*

The charcoal remnants were left in the camper's grill. Many of them were unburned, completely untouched by the fire. Another example of man's wastefulness. The economy of our nation seems to be built on waste. *In the economy of God there is no waste.*

The Bible illustrates this truth by giving us models (object lessons) in both the Old and the New Testaments. For instance, in Exodus 25 in the instructions for the design and care of the tabernacle and its furnishings there is a significant line that tells us much about God's economy. Note that even the burnt trimmings of the lamp wicks used in the tabernacle were to be saved (Exod. 25:38a). Surely God is saying to His people already by such a prescribed practice early in their history: "In my house (or household) nothing goes to waste. Everything must and will be saved."

Such is one of the models God provides for showing us how His economy operates—there is no waste. Follow the teaching through as you read the Bible and you will discover many unusual models for teaching and so much comfort for daily living. Read Psalm 56 and note how David, when suffering battle fatigue, draws upon this comfort of God's meticulous, preserving care and in so doing, he can confidently go back to his assigned task.

David cries in his distress, "O God . . . put thou my tears in thy bottle!" Every tear? Yes, every single drop God notices and saves. Likely the figure of a tear-bottle is drawn from the history of the Israelites—something borrowed from the tradition of Egypt, a place where David's ancestors lived for many years. The first tears of an Egyptian child were put into a bottle and buried with the body. (Such tear-bottles have been discovered by archaeologists.) So David prays, "God, save my tears!"

And God replies, "I will! Remember, I taught your fathers, when I gave them the pattern for my house, to save everything, even the scraps of a burned wick. And I am the same God. My ways do not change. I will save every tear and bury your tear-bottle with your body. Then some day I'll raise up your body and together we'll throw that tear-bottle away."

And David dried his tears (but note that he had shed them) and said: "With You to help me, O God, I can face anything. You save, You help, You strengthen! Thanks, thanks ever so much for being my God today and always."

Then David sang again: "And in that light of life I'll walk 'til traveling days are done."

39

God Keeps a Record

Scripture: John 6:1-13; 37-39; Malachi 3:16-4:3a; Psalm 103

> *"And this is the will of him who sent me, that I should lose nothing of all that he has given me, but raise it up at the last day" (John 6:39, RSV).*
>
> *". . . And a book of remembrance was written before him of those who feared the Lord and thought on his name. 'They shall be mine,' says the Lord of hosts, 'my special possession on the day when I act, and I will spare them as a man spares his son who serves him' " (Mal. 3:16b-17, RSV)*

Every teacher knows the tedium and the discipline involved in keeping records. We record attendance, grades, test scores, health conditions, and similar data about our students.

God, too, has a record book, and He keeps book really well. He has only gains—no losses. He keeps all his possessions with special care. Nothing is wasted in God's economy.

To make this point very clear, Christ gave an object lesson. (I am becoming more and more aware of the many carefully designed models the Lord uses for our instruction.) In the feeding of the five thousand, all the scraps of food had to be picked up—every single bit. Later (John 6:37-39) Jesus explained the significance of this act—". . . that I should lose nothing of all that the Father has given me . . ." So, those who come to Christ become His "special possession" (Mal. 3:17) and He keeps a very special record of them.

What's in God's record book? First of all, our names. ". . . My fellow workers, whose names are in the book of life" (Phil. 4:3b, RSV). Take a moment to picture your name as it is written in God's book. And note well: there are no erasures in God's book. "He who overcomes . . . I will never erase his name from the book of life" (Rev. 3:5a, NIV).

Any health record or record of a "physical" lately? We scan the page carefully and note that all the parts of our bodies were listed in God's book before they were formed! "Thou didst see my limbs unformed in the womb, and in thy book they are all recorded" (Ps. 139:16a, NEB). Amazing! Incredible! Take a moment to think about that.

Now we look at the record again, rather excitedly this time, to see whether there are any special comments behind each name. Sure enough! All our struggles, our heartaches, our sleepless nights are on record.

> "Thou hast kept count of my tossings . . .
> Are they not in thy book?" (Ps. 56:8, RSV).

O God, what a record book You keep! Nothing overlooked. Nothing wasted. My name is in it; every detail about my body and my griefs and fears are recorded. But what about my sins, Lord?

And God says, "Turn the page." There it is—a big red X. And written in large letters across the record is one word: FORGIVEN! Down at the bottom is the little word *over*. And on the last page in God's book of life are these words: REJOICE! CELEBRATE!

40

A Little Bit of Heaven on Earth

Scripture: Psalm 104

> *"O Lord my God, thou art great indeed,*
> *clothed in majesty and splendour . . ." (Ps. 104:1b, NEB)*

I heard a message on heaven recently and it was beautiful. Yet, I wanted to add, "Heaven is here and now, too." I really believe that, and I invite you to believe and to see it with me.

At dinner with one of my students last night, she said, "Do you know what I remember as two of the best classes in all my school days? "One was the day of 'the storm,' when the sky was an awesome color and hailstones like small baseballs were falling all around us. And you let us go to the window—just to watch the storm."

She continued, as I listened, wondering what the second most memorable lesson was, "The other time was that first exceptionally clear spring day when you said, 'The view from where I sit is so resplendent today I should not be the only one in this class enjoying it. Just turn your chairs around and enjoy it with me throughout this hour.' " (I recall that day, too, and from that classroom we could see all the splendor of the valleys and the mountains in their spring colors—even the Smokies in the distance.)

You, too, can seize psychological moments for fresh views and times to let imagination play so that you and your students can experience a little bit of heaven on earth. Then, because we've had real glimpses of heaven in this life, we will be able to sing more truly and expectantly:

> My God, how wonderful Thou art!
> Thy majesty, how bright! . . .
> What rapture will it be . . .
> To . . . gaze and gaze on Thee!
>
> Frederick Faber

41

"Images of Stillness"

Scripture: Psalm 23

> *"He makes me to lie down in green pastures;*
> *He leads me beside restful water;*
> *He revives my soul . . ." (Ps. 23:2-3, Berkeley).*

As an antidote to the pressures of certain days at school, I often dream of quieting things—"images of stillness." The well-known "shepherd's psalm" uses such restful and refreshing images. This psalm so caught the imagination of a young Japanese Christian that she wrote the following parody on it:

The Lord is my Pace-Setter, I shall not rush.

He makes me stop for quiet intervals; He provides me with images of stillness, which restore my serenity.

He leads me in ways of efficiency through calmness of mind, and His guidance is peace.

Even though I have a great many things to accomplish each day, I will not fret, for His presence is here.

His timeliness, His all-importance, will keep me in balance.

He prepares refreshments and renewal in the midst of my activity by anointing my mind with His oil of tranquility; My cup of joyous energy overflows.

Surely harmony and effectiveness shall be the fruit of my hours, and I shall walk in the peace of the Lord and dwell in His House forever.

Toki Miyashina

A retiring professor from the University of Pittsburgh recommended in his farewell address: "We ought to revise our curricula so that we take only one course per semester. Then we ought to take a course in Quietness each term—Quietness I, Quietness II, etc. This course would require the student to sit in solitude for at least two hours a day with no books or papers around. Under such an arrangement perhaps college students—and teachers—might learn something at the end of four years." He went on to say something like this: "Isn't it strange that in our rush and concern to explore the moon nowadays very few of us take time to look at the stars!"

"Images of stillness" . . . "green pastures" . . . "restful waters" revive souls. Revive yourself by quieting yourself and dreaming a little.

> There is a river whose streams
> make glad the city of God,
> the holy dwelling of the Most High.

> God is in her midst;
> she shall not totter;
> at morning's dawn God shall help her.

> Nations rage, kingdoms fall;
> He raises His voice,
> the earth dissolves.

> Be still and know that I am God.

> (Ps. 46:4-6, 10, Berkeley)

42

Keep Your Giving Secret

Scripture: Matthew 6:1-4

> *"But when you give alms, do not let your left hand know what your right hand is doing" (Matt. 6:3, RSV).*

Advertise! Advertise! This is the shout of the world today. There is a legitimate place for telling people honestly and clearly what to see and what to buy. In the case of giving, however, Christ's command is quite the opposite. He says in effect, "Don't advertise your deeds of mercy and giving. Don't let even your inner self know and remember."

Just recently I saw something of the meaning of Christ's words and the wisdom in them. In order to make myself plain and to help you gain insight into Christ's strange command, I'll have to tell you something which at another time would be better kept secret or at least not widely known.

Last week my friend was carrying a $50 bill in her purse, the first one she had ever had. Two days later she heard an appeal in chapel for a special love-gift for a needy student. She felt moved to give that $50 anonymously. Later in the week she wondered what she had done with the money but did not feel disturbed about it. Then she recalled that she had given the money away on an impulse "at the impulse of Christ's love"—about which we sing readily but act upon rarely lest we be labelled "impulsive." And she thanked God for the freedom to give and then to forget about it.

As my reflections on secret giving continued, I wondered how many people have given responsibly and yet almost un-wittingly—forgetfully. I think teachers are in a beautiful position to do just that—to give and then forget about just what they have given and to whom. There is something so wonderful about having opportunities to invest in people quietly and faithfully every day. And it's wonderful to know that such giving goes far beyond any recognition this world has to offer, for "your Father who sees what is done in secret will reward you."

43

Ask God Some Questions

Scripture: Psalm 13

> *"How long, O Lord, wilt thou quite forget me?"*
> *"How long must I suffer anguish in my soul?"* (Ps. 13:1a,
> 2a, NEB).

There are times in the lives of all of us when disappointments and frustrations almost knock us out. Disappointment hit me hard today. I had anticipated receiving a letter, but when it came, it caused distress and pain, rather than relief. I wept. I cried all through my lunch hour and wondered how I was going to meet my classes in the afternoon. I hurt all over but especially in the heart.

Then I recalled that somewhere in the Psalms there was a record of similar distress. I thought it was Psalm 13, and it was. I read it through twice and found in it just what I needed. I like that psalm because the writer dares to ask God some questions. He lists the specific things that are troubling him and addresses his questions directly to God. I did just that and found the exercise very helpful. Some of the questions still remain, but now they're in God's hands and on His mind—not mine.

In times past I recall being told that man ought not question God. It is more accurate to say, I believe, that we ought not to doubt God, but we surely may and should ask Him some questions. The Bible is full of men's questions. Even the Lord Jesus cried out, "My God, *why.* . . ?" And really, how can God ever answer us if we never ask Him any questions?

So, I recommend to you to let God know when you hurt and tell Him exactly how you feel by asking Him some specific questions. He listens because He cares.

44

Expect God's Answers

Scripture: Psalm 13

> *"If you call to me I will answer you, and tell you great and mysterious things which you do not understand"* (Jer. 33:2b, NEB).
>
> *"Thou dost guide me by thy counsel . . ."* (Ps. 73:24b, NEB).

I was too tired yesterday to see straight. Now after some rest and after addressing some of my questions directly to God, I think my vision is about back to normal. At least, my perspective is clearer and brighter.

From the depths of my frustration I asked God yesterday, "What are You doing to me? I sought a new place, prayerfully. Now I have that offer, but the terms seem so demeaning. Must I start at the *bottom* again?"

This morning God set me straight—firmly but kindly. "Quiet down, Nelle. Just go about your work cheerfully, thankfully, and faithfully. All that is required of a steward is that he be found faithful. Live according to my criteria day by day, step by step, and I, your God, will guide and reward you."

Thank You, Lord. I'm so glad You're in control. Now I can sing again with the psalmist. I couldn't come to that point last night, but I can now. And what am I singing? A song that used to trouble me. I often felt hypocritical singing it—but not this morning:

> My Jesus, I love Thee;
> I know Thou art mine . . .
> I'll love Thee in life;
> I will love Thee in death;
> And praise Thee as long
> As Thou lendest me breath.

Yes, ask God questions and then expect God's loving answers. God is love, and He cares—He *really* cares. Believe it! Believe it with all your heart. And go on your way rejoicing. What could ever go wrong?

45

My Strength and Song

Scripture: Psalm 27, Psalm 118

"The Lord is my strength and my song; he has become my salvation" (Ps. 118:14, RSV).

> The Lord is my light and my salvation;
> whom, then, shall I fear?
> The Lord is the strength of my life;
> of whom, then, shall I be afraid?

That song based on Psalm 27 that I heard in chapel this morning is still ringing in my ears.

The Lord gave the song, and He also prepared the special singer for this song today. Patty, born and reared in Peru as the child of missionaries and also trained in nursing, has known much suffering. But she has always been known among us as our "singing nurse." She has blessed so many lives by her radiant smile and by her buoyant spirit—by her "light" and her "strength." The singer and the song are one. O Lord, how beautiful!

Thanks, thanks ever so much, Lord, for such beauty. How beautiful heaven must be!

Help us all, as we trudge through the sands of time and toil to keep our eyes upon the stars, that one star especially, the Lord who is our Light. May we also draw upon Your strength each step of the way. And help us to sing and to teach others to sing, with growing conviction and joy, "The Lord is my light . . . The Lord is the strength of my life."

46

Reflections on "Tired Feet"

Scripture: Luke 14:7-11

"So let us never tire of doing good, for if we do not slacken our efforts we shall in due time reap our harvest" (Gal. 6:9, NEB).

In recent years I am more and more amazed at how neatly the Lord brings things together in our lives and at how "wonder-full" His ways and His timing are. I think I am learning to fret less (though I slip seriously still) and to rest more. I'm learning to let God take care of me with the confidence that He loves me and is steadily working toward making me lovely—like Jesus Him-self.

My reflections and amazement were prompted anew by a simply beautiful farewell gift from my colleagues—an unusual woodcut done in delicate colors with unusual subjects: a pair of army boots on the left and a box of coleus (plants) in the center and on the right. The work of art was produced by one of my colleagues and was selected especially for me by the people who have worked most closely with me in recent years. And then it was presented to me without any fanfare and without any or-namentation at a simple, but lovely, homecooked buffet supper. Everything was so simple, so comfortable, so beautiful. Love, so much genuine, deep love was in it all. I responded with simple thanks but with much more inner emotion than I dared to reveal.

Are your feet tired? Do as my painting suggests. Kick off your shoes and look at a fresh, delicately-colored plant. Reflect on God's ways and God's works in you, through you, and around you. You will be refreshed and thankful. *Power comes from being quiet with God.*

"Bless the Lord, my soul:
O Lord my God, thou art great indeed . . ." (Ps. 104:1, NEB).

47

The Benediction

Scripture: Hebrews 13; Numbers 6:22-27; Psalm 80, 89

> *"May the God of peace who brought again from the dead our Lord Jesus, the great shepherd of the sheep, by the blood of the eternal covenant, equip you with everything good that you may do his will, working in you that which is pleasing in his sight, through Jesus Christ; to whom be glory for ever and ever. Amen"* (Heb. 13:20-21, RSV).

> *"The Lord bless you and keep you:*
> *The Lord make his face to shine upon you,*
> *and be gracious to you:*
> *The Lord lift up his countenance upon you,*
> *and give you peace"* (Num. 6:24-26, RSV).

Take five minutes right now to read, re-read, and reflect on the above texts. Having done so, you will never be quite the same, and you will go on thinking about them.

I put my academic garb away today, carefully, for many memories were being folded away with it. I'm leaving a place that I love, people I've grown fond of, warm fellowships with students and colleagues, and blessed opportunities to work. I was sad yesterday. And yet as I walked in the recessional at the side of a special friend, I was also glad and I could smile. I think I felt a bit of what it is to exchange the black gown of earth for the white robe of heaven.

The words that gave me such a flash of insight and lifted me from sadness to gladness were those in the above texts. They were expressed so firmly and yet so tenderly by an esteemed friend and colleague. I'll never forget that moment and those words. They will stay with me always in a very special way. Again, it has come home to me that the benedictions (blessings) of the Lord are not wishes but facts.

And today as I reflect upon those words, the speaker, and the occasion, I can only say, "O Lord, my God, how great You are! You led me to this place some years ago. You used the prayer of

Dr. S. to persuade me to come. Now You send me forth to another field of service with Your blessing spoken by the same man."

My heart is full of song today. One song after another comes to mind and flows from my mouth. O God, grant that:

> My song forever shall record
> The tender mercies of the Lord;

And as I go from place to place, may the theme of my teachings be constant:

> Thy faithfulness will I proclaim,
> And [so that] every age shall know Thy name.
>
> Ps. 89:1 (metrical version)

48

Treasures in Heaven

Scripture: Matthew 6:19-24

> *". . . store up for yourselves treasures in heaven. For where your treasure is, there your heart will be also"* (Matt. 6:20, 21, NIV).

Have you ever had to declare all of your assets, that is, exactly how much of this world's goods you might have to pass on to others? Recently I discovered that what I had as a will had been illegal for four years. I decided I ought to get business in better order. When the lawyer asked me to list approximately what my assets were, I was embarrassed. I had very little to declare, and I said, almost apologetically, "Not much, is it? I guess I've been investing in people most of my life and my return on such investments can't be listed."

He responded so quietly that he startled me when he said, "What better investment could you have? Money and power are still the most corrupting influences in this world." Such a comment prompted me to inquire a bit into the man's sense of values and his innermost commitments. And he, in turn, was very curious about my commitment and my reasons for staying in Christian teaching. In the end we spent a most profitable hour together—twenty minutes making up my will and the rest of the time discussing what really counts in life.

On the way home and many times thereafter, I've come back to that encounter, and I realize how the Lord put me on the spot that morning to help me reassess my values. I've thanked the Lord for that confrontation. I'm beginning to see that one of the ways to "store up treasures in heaven" is to *invest* in *people* here on earth. People—your students and mine—"do not rust." as things do. People are treasures—lasting treasures. And it's fun—sheer delight—to seize opportunities for investing whatever the Lord has given in the hearts and lives of others. Also, I find increasingly, and no doubt many of you do, too, that by making such investments my heart is really in my work, for it *is* just as Christ said, "Where your treasure is, there will your heart be also."

49

Dailiness

Scripture: Nehemiah 1, Psalm 145

> *"Grant me good success this day, and put it into this man's heart to show me kindness" (Neh. 1:11b, NEB).*
> *"Every day will I bless thee" (Ps. 145:2a, NEB).*
> *". . . joy in the Lord is your strength" (Neh. 8:10b, NEB).*
> *"Look towards him and shine with joy" (Ps. 34:5a, NEB).*

> Look to this day!
> For it is life . . .
> Yesterday is but a dream,
>   And tomorrow is only a vision;
> But today, well lived,
>   makes every yesterday
> a dream of happiness,
> And every tomorrow
> a vision of hope.
> Look well, therefore,
>   to this day!

> Salutation to the Dawn translated
> from the Sanskrit

I like the lilt and the music of those words and a bit of its simple philosophy. I suspect I could not live on these thoughts from day to day, however, because they lack the essence of daily living—"eye contact" between God and me. I need the assurance each day that God is looking at me lovingly and faithfully. And He wants me to look to him every day—lovingly and expectantly.

Nehemiah is one of the best examples in Scripture of daily "on-the-job" contact with the Lord. His job, while in captivity, was to serve wine to the king. The work was not so simple as it may sound, for the cupbearer had to be very alert to guard against poisoning the king. A responsible job, but not glamorous. Furthermore, a cupbearer was expected always to look pleasant. And we all know that there are times when a genuinely cheerful look is impossible.

How did Nehemiah handle this job? He prayed; he was constantly in touch with God. He prayed before the day began. Read one of his morning prayers in Nehemiah 1. It's so real, so specific, so down-to-earth. And he prayed as the day progressed, right in the midst of his work. Before he replied to the king's question: "Why do you look so unhappy today"? he sent another "SOS" to heaven. "I prayed to the God of heaven, and then I answered . . ." (Neh. 2:5).

Prayer marked every step of Nehemiah's route from cupbearer in exile to wall-builder in Jerusalem. And as he built the walls, faced the enemy, and revived a nation, he prayed his way through every day. And God strengthened his hand and gladdened his heart, day by day.

Read Nehemiah for a shining example of godly dailiness and you will find with him that "joy in the Lord is your strength" (Neh. 8:10b).

Day by Day

Day by day, and with each passing moment,
Strength I find to meet my trials here;
Trusting in my Father's wise bestowment,
I've no cause for worry or for fear.
He, whose heart is kind beyond all measure,
Gives unto each day what He deems best,
Lovingly its part of pain and pleasure,
Mingling toil with peace and rest.
Ev'ry day the Lord Himself is near me,
With a special mercy for each hour;
All my cares He fain would bear and cheer me,
He whose name is Counsellor and Pow'r.
The protection of His child and treasure
Is a charge that on Himself He laid;
"As thy days, thy strength shall be in measure,"
This is the pledge to me He made.

Lina Sandell

50

Lead by Stepping Aside

Scripture: Matthew 19:13-14

> *"Jesus said, 'Let the little children come to me, and do not hinder them" (Matt. 19:14a, NIV).*
> *"Nothing gives me greater joy than to hear that my children are living by the truth" (III John 4, NEB).*

The time comes in teachers' lives (and in the lives of everyone) to teach their last lesson to a particular group. For such a time I chose to read the following parable to my students in children's literature.

A Parable

I took a little child's hand in mine. He and I were to walk together for a while. I was to lead him to the Father. It was a task that overcame me, so awful was the responsibility. And so I talked to the child only of the Father. I painted the sternness of His face were the child to do something to displease him. I spoke of the child's goodness as something that would appease the Father's wrath. We walked under the tall trees. I said the Father has power to send them crashing down, struck by His thunderbolts. We walked in the sunshine, I told him of the greatness of the Father, who makes the burning, blazing sun. And one twilight we met the Father. The child hid behind me. He was afraid. He would not take the Father's hand. I was between the child and the Father. I wondered. I had been so conscientious, so serious.

* * *

I took a little child's hand in mine. I was to lead him to the Father. I felt burdened with the multiplicity of the things I had to teach him. We did not ramble; we hastened from spot to spot. At one moment we compared the leaves of different trees. In the next we were examining a bird's nest. While the child was questioning me about it, I hurried him away to chase a butterfly. Did he chance to fall asleep, I awakened him, lest he should miss something I wished him to see. We

79

spoke of the Father, oh, yes, often and rapidly. I poured into his ears all the stories he ought to know, but we were interrupted often by the wind a-blowing, of which we needs must study; by the gurgling of a brook which we must trace to its source, then, in the twilight, we met the Father. The child merely glanced at Him, and then his gaze wandered in a dozen directions. The Father stretched out His hand. The child was not interested enough to take it. Feverish spots burned his cheeks. He dropped exhausted to the ground and fell asleep. Again I was between the child and the Father. I wondered. I had taught him so many things.

* * *

I took a little child's hand to lead him to the Father. My heart was full of gratitude for the glad privilege. We walked slowly. I suited my steps to the short steps of the child. We spoke of the things the child noticed. Sometimes we picked the Father's flowers and stroked their soft petals and loved their bright colors. Sometimes it was one of the Father's birds. We watched it build its nest. We saw the eggs that were laid. We wondered later at the care it gave its young. Often we told stories of the Father. I told them to the child, and the child told them again to me. We told them, the child and I, over and over again. Sometimes we stopped to rest, leaning against one of the Father's trees, and letting His cool air cool our brows, and never speaking. And then, in the twilight, we met the Father. The child's eyes shone, He looked lovingly, trustingly, eagerly up into the Father's face. He put his hand into the Father's Hand. I was for the moment forgotten. I was content.

Reflection Reading: Read the letters of John this week three times. The first time just read them through aloud. (This can be done in twenty to thirty minutes). The next time underline the word *children* each time it appears in these letters. The third time, take time to see the Father with open eyes, and more of your place as His child as it is revealed (unveiled) to you. Fresh insights and new vision guaranteed!